50 Windows

Niketa Mulay

BookLeaf Publishing

India | USA | UK

Presentation by *BookLeaf Publishing*

Web: www.bookleafpub.com

E-mail: info@bookleafpub.com

ISBN: 9789360940928

First edition 2024

CONTENTS

ACKNOWLEDGEMENT
PREFACE
At Dawn

The Mother | 1
Ritual | 2
Morning tea on the terrace | 3
Thawing an existence | 4
A crumpled grocery list | 6
No two greys are the same | 7
Dying without scars | 9
Carnations in the rain | 11
Just a little broken | 12
Gossamer | 13

The Morning Goes By

Metropolis | 15
Who do I speak to? | 16
Decay | 18
The door | 20
All poetry is protest | 23
Don't touch me | 25
In the heart of art | 27
Centipede's atlas | 29
As old as my… | 30
Mending | 32

Afternoon Showers

Tea | 35
Look up | 36
An afternoon to spare | 38

The room that smells of you   39
An old house   40
Community   41
Two pieces of luggage   42
Social insanity   43
Dirty   45

Eventide

Filling up an empty cup   47
Cut the cord   49
China cups in the sink   50
Pink   51
The sights of Manora   52
Forgotten umbrellas   54
Favourite colour   55
Fervent catharsis   56
Ageing   58
Aloneness   59

Nightlife

Last light   61
Reflections   62
Dinner time   63
Lunatic   64
Giving up the race   66
Rebirth   67
Hear the stars   68
Sleepwalking   69
Wishes at midnight   70
Time for silence   72
Cradling the radio   73

ACKNOWLEDGEMENT

The process of writing poetry and publishing it are two very different and almost opposite activities. While writing these poems was deeply personal for me, publishing them made me vulnerable to the various interpretations.

For encouraging me to publish them, I am grateful to my husband Ranjit, my son Vikrant and a dear departed friend, Rakesh Kaushik. I finally gave in to their constant nagging and decided to set the caged words free on the breeze for the world.

PREFACE

Imagine a city awash with rain, a concrete jungle under a grey sky. We walk its bustling streets, not as participants but as observers. This collection of poems is an invitation to peer through fifty windows, each a fleeting glimpse into the lives unfolding within.

From the soft glow of dawn to the neon hum of night, these poems capture the kaleidoscope of human experience. We witness love drenched in doubt, loneliness echoing in a solitary room. We catch glimpses of societal struggles, the echoes of past traumas, and a yearning for connection steeped in nostalgia.

Nature, too, finds its way into these frames, a reminder of the beauty that persists even amidst the urban sprawl.

But, above all, these poems are the whispers we catch, the fleeting glimpses that ignite the fire of our own introspection. We eavesdrop on the internal dialogues, the unspoken desires, and the quiet battles fought within the walls of each illuminated frame.

Welcome, then, to a journey through the city's soul. Prepare to be surprised, touched, and challenged as you peer through the fifty windows, each a portal to the complex and multifaceted tapestry of life.

AT DAWN

The Mother

She is here, and she stays.
The setting moon, a silver coin, rests on her
brow
She looks at me through her dark veil,
The gentle breeze is her breath.
The quietness is her hand on my head
saying, be peaceful.

As the birds wake up one by one
they greet her presence with a soft trill.
Everything is her;
I am her, and she is me,
A reflection in the stream,
I want to hold on to these precious moments—
before the Sun blushes in the East,
before the night vanishes,
before the light creeps in.

I am warm in her presence;
this cold breeze is cleansing me.
She gently transcends into her new self
as the sky changes from dark to blue,
and then the golden rays greet her through their
sleepy eyes.
She smiles.

Ritual

Tapping sounds of the stove
Aroma of tea leaves
mixes with the faint smell of kerosene.

Last night's bread on a chipped white saucer
With an empty tea cup, rests in anticipation.
Early morning moon sets on the quiet horizon
The sun is yet to come out.

A ritual of dimming lights
and quiet hopes tiptoe together,
Just an hour before the sea of chaos resumes
Its ebb and flow, twice a day.

Morning tea on the terrace

Ripples dance on the surface,
of the water collected on the black granite.
They move in a crazed, intermittent rhythm that
I can't hear;
It's a secret between the wind and the water
and I can only feel its after-effects.

The dance of the ripples distorts everything
reflected in its world:
the water tank, the palm tree, the crow, and me.
No one is left behind; things are like they
shouldn't be,
Because my world is made of no such dances of
whim,
Merely straight lines which I have been taught to
colour within.

Now the palm is dancing, and
the ripples reach a climax
of perfect harmony with the wind,
Droplets escape the surface and seek my face;
I gaze into this alternate world to escape my
own.

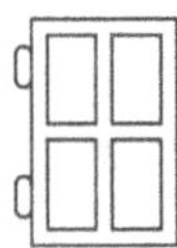

Thawing an existence

The morning light filtered into a dingy bedroom
through a maze of high-rises right outside.
The sounds of people getting busy with their
lives
pervade my quiet temple.

I strain my ears to hear the few mynahs
twittering;
Their shrill, high-pitched sounds rise above
the ambulance wailing, the rickshaw spewing
smoke,
and the superbike speeding past:
And I lighten my heavy heart at last.

Routine is a magical thing;
I need the routine of waking up to check if my
son is still sleeping,
Check the clock on the bright screen of my
phone,
Check if I can stand up without pain in my left
foot,
And check again if, by some trick, you are back
home.

The routine reassures me that life isn't falling to
pieces;

I speak often to hear my own voice,
I laugh readily to ease that weight within.
The only thing that makes me feel complete is
when I see your smiling eyes, your gentle face,
and your firm hands that hold me close.

I return to the growing light in my bedroom,
The old earthen pot outside the window has a
few buds,
Thawing an existence,
I wait for them to bloom.

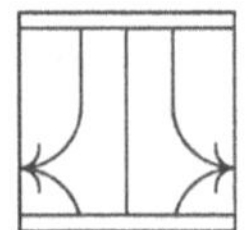

A crumpled grocery list

A crumpled grocery list,
the ink fading like my grasp on the day.
Am I alone?
Besides a photo of the past
And no relevance of it in the present
I keep this memory with me
Like old grocery lists in my wallet
That have no use except to remind me of what I
needed before.

A sunrise of the same kind
Puts me in a mood
because it smells like good food
on a familiar table.
I welcome this sense of belonging
With the reluctance of an amnesiac
With the hope that I might remember more
someday.

No two greys are the same

When the clouds came,
I asked them to paint my sky
In hues that were so variedly grey
Like shades of time on an antique silver tray.

When the clouds came,
They dusted the sky with cotton tufts
Dabbed with powdered clay
That hung like drapes all puffed up and heavy
And the early rays filtered through them.

When the clouds came,
They sang for me in boisterous tones of
thundering bass
Baritones that echoed till far,
they laughed like the roughnecks in an inn
Drunk by the rain they held.

When the clouds came,
I ran to greet them, and they welcomed me
With a crack of light that tore the grey
And towered above the translucent sheets that
fell
In a rhythmic dance with a deafening sound.

When the clouds came,
All was quiet
Inside my head that spun around
And my thoughts that spoke in incessant chatter
Were silenced by the roaring outside.

When the clouds came,
The wind swirled around the dust
That gathered in my stuffy heart
And when it quietened in my mind
They gave me a rainbow.

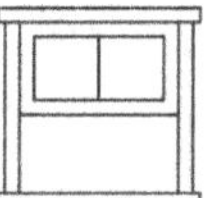

Dying without scars

In the dull light of a rainy morning
The satin negligee slipped down her skin.
She avoided the mirror,
it's been long since their relationship ended;
Some things are better terminated,
When there is nothing that they can give each
other.
The mirror loved her once, and she loved it
back.

Scars, they say, may not run deep but hurt
deeply.
The scars were badges of achievement,
they never hurt her the way she was troubled
now;
Back from the field, when she looked at herself
she knew what each scar stood for.

Some were fresh, some from before,
and they kept telling her the stories in her head.
The mirror spoke to her about every welt and
cut,
About every gunshot pierced, deafening booms,
charred skin, and pounding breath.

She returned to the chaos through the mirror and
found herself amidst the ruins,
The clamour to run for shelter and the struggle
to stay awake.
She belonged there, with the others,
not here where the yellow chrysanthemum
made friends with the peace lily on the window
sill.
She couldn't make friends with her lover, her
mother, her neighbour.
Her mirror kept her protected, safe in the place
she had come from.

Her satin negligee formed an 'O' where it slipped
down,
She looked at the pills on the countertop,
A prescription said she had to take them thrice a
day for thirty days.
Twenty down, ten still left,
her relationship with the mirror is broken
She can't go back;

The scars are fading, and so is she.

Carnations in the rain

The carnations drenched in raindrops
Reflect her mind deluged with the wetness
of days in the falling rain.
While anxiously awaiting the first kiss,
the carnations witnessed her joy in soaked
clothes on the rooftop with him,
And shyly swayed with the breeze that sent a
shiver through her body.

An umbilical was broken,
She moved out of the shell of being untouched,
unfelt and unseen;
The flames within were fanned by the shower
outside,
That day, it rained like never before.

The carnations still sway in the breeze,

Only now, they witness grey skies and rain
But no kiss, no shiver, no flame;
Just the walls remain that bear the mossy marks
of water dripping steadily;
They stand around, revealing the age and
remnants of memories.

Just a little broken

Just a little broken
A few loose screws here and there
Under different circumstances
Chances could have been fair.

I don't intend to hurt
But things go awry
Did you see the sunshine
Light up my way?
Fuel is running low
I didn't see it go
My eyes were set afar
But the ground was hungry below.

It will swallow me soon
To ashes, I will burn
Alas, the phoenix could rise
I have no chance of return.

A solo flight of a mad man
They will say this henceforth
But before I die, I shall smile
For freedom, this flight was worth.

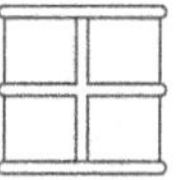

Gossamer

Gossamer;
I like the way the word feels when I say it
It slips on the sly through my teeth
As I catch it with my lips
And let go again with my breath into the ether.

Spun fine and delicate
The fragile pattern shivers
in the misty monsoon morning.
Reflecting the sun's rays
like tiny specks of gold and glimmer,
My eyes stare at this transient wonder.
Hear it whisper on the breeze, a secret gently
writ.
Catching the first light's embrace,
ethereal, it clings to a blade of grace.

Gossamer;
Very few words can sound
the way they feel to your touch
Slipping through my mouth like ether.

THE MORNING GOES BY

Metropolis

So, the noisy streets of the city beckoned me
And I came wearing a smile of familiarity.
I came home to a surprising chaos
Where every element had its purpose:
The sirens wailing at all times at the busy
junction;
Honking cars rushing with the clock;
The smell of cement and water on a newly paved
road;
People consuming, living, talking and walking
through this maze of lights, roads, and half-done
bridges.

Surreal, but true.
This den of din, this city of sin
Has the virtue of embracing everyone in its fold,
The young, the rich, the poor, and the old.
Its colonial gems are like the heirlooms that are
sparkled with care
Its coastline is omnipresent like the air
The people shift and move like the sea
Disrupting and constructing masses of humanity.

Who do I speak to?

Who do I speak to?
A narrow window to a world so removed
Stands open, devoid of any people
To speak with or be spoken to.

I search and seek
In words so bleak
A lot is being shared
But nothing is said.

A mute world with a deaf populace
Only sighted enough to watch,
Like a voyeur into other lives
Of strangers, dogs and cooking with chives.

Lift your head and say hello
Look up, a friendly face is hollow,
Comfort, connect and share a few words
In this age of faceless books and untwittering
birds.

I hear no familiar voices,
Just images on the internet.
The fake plastic smiles
Selling sex, food and lies.

Are you still stuck like glue
to that tool on a cue?
Can't you hear that knocking
On your door, that's shocking!

Someone has come to say
Why don't you step away;
Come walk with me, explore and see,
The real world's beauty waiting to be.

Decay

It spreads...
At first, slow, gradually seeping
It's the stink of humanity rotting.
Grabbing minds that are void
Of thoughts and ideas devoid.

It spreads...
Segregation on a factory line
Branding, colouring to pick or assign.
You Hindu, you woman, you labourer,
You? You don't really matter.

It spreads...
The fetid stench is reeking
With the blood of innocents seeking
Justice for their meek souls
In this carious society full of holes.

It spreads...
Riding on the wind, it calls
With false hope of change, it appals
Faceless enemy, some may say
Look around; the stench gives them away.

Every move is calculated,
Every penny is accounted,

Every caste is noted
Every thumbprint recorded.
Every word is accorded
A shade that matches their view.

Mediocrity hails,
intelligence wails
Poor are numb,
rich wiggle their thumb,
Wagers slog,
employers flog,
And with all of this,
The big bosses watch.

The door

She rang the bell, drenched
Riding through the lashing rain
With one thought alone:
Will he be home?

Seconds tick by till she hears
From the other side
The sound of a chair dragged
The feet shifting and then,
Click, the latch turns.

She wills the wooden door
To stay stuck and shut.
Her thoughts, like her clothes
Are soaked in the agony
Of facing her desire and fighting her rational
mind.

A crack opens in the brown rectangle
That's as big and wide
As the trunk of the huge tropical tree
She once tried to hug in vain
On a holiday somewhere.

She shivers slightly,
the cool draft that blew through the crack

Makes her conscious of her wet skin
While inside her body
The lava of a thousand thoughts
Run through her veins;
She feels thankful for the rain.

A shadow shifts along the light
In the partly opened door,
She sees hands fiddling with a chain
Which reminds her of the ones in her life.

A creaky hinge makes groaning sounds
Her mind translates it to the open jaws
Of a crocodile prepared to devour its prey;
But here, who is who,
How can she say?

She decides to abort the plan
Run away before he can
'Coz rejection is the last straw
That will destroy her faith
In the magnetism of serendipity.

But before she can walk away
He sees her turning figure
And calls out her name
In a voice dripping with anticipation.

She stops in her tracks,
And the tiny pools formed around her feet
drown her.

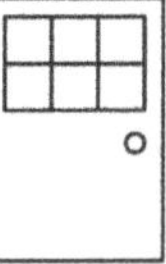

All poetry is protest

All poetry is protest…
A protest against keeping feelings bottled up
A protest against the mind telling you to shut up
A protest against the norm
A protest to stand up to a storm.

Each line, a battle cry against the mundane,
A protest against a world restrained,
Breaking barriers, norms, and the status quo,
Unveiling the truths I've come to know.

It defies the notion of keeping it in,
Those bottled feelings that weigh me within,
Through rhythmic verses, they find their release,
A cathartic rebellion, a sense of peace.

The mind may whisper, "Your words are in vain,
Keep silent, conform, surrender to the strain."
But poetry resists, refuses to obey,
It raises its voice, demanding its say.

With every syllable, it breaks the rusted locks,
A dormant spirit finally wakes and walks.
In the tapestry of verses, it finds liberation,
For poetry, at its core, is a protestation.

So let your pens dance, your voices resound,
In the realm of poetry, let our truths be found.
A protest against silence, a bold declaration,
For all poetry is a form of righteous indignation.

Don't touch me

Touch, touch, touch,
we all like to touch.
Some touch to love, some touch to hate,
some touch to care, some touch for faith.
Some touch to kill, for vigilantism, saffronism,
and bloody hell hedonism.
In an auto, in a train, in a market, in vain.

We touch, touch, touch.
No matter the cause,
we don't stop,
we don't pause,
to think before a hand is raised,
in striking, in hitting, mob mentality shakes our
brains.

When feeling up her skirt or touching her
breasts,
we applaud our masochism, thumping our chest.
Bullshitting, ogling, bludgeoning insane, we
touch to feel like a man again.

We spare no thought to the drought
that's bought
as she sells herself to the nought
that got caught
in the skewed socio-political game.

Coz we love to touch...
touch the raw nerve of a naive viewer,
crass commercials making us dumber,
lost in phones, a lonely crowd, move around,
move aside, move beside,
push, pull, jerk, feel
and so, again, turns the wheel.

In the heart of art

Art is the toddler's red brick scribbles on the
white-washed walls of my village house,
Art is the Baul's serenade I hear across the
fields,
Art is the warmth of the patchwork quilt made
from my grandmother's muslin saree,
Art is the neighbour's crisscross rangoli.

An image was conjured and lost to the potter's
hands,
They worked in tandem with his thoughts,
And poured his heart into the vessel that he
created,
A part of his being.
An art of his existence.

My eyes learn to see beyond the start
From the childhood scribbles to the potter's art
Art whispers in a language I now know
And hope to fathom the depths of this fevered
trance.

Why not express rather than bother to define;
Like love, art spreads its wings far
And dwells in the mind like a lover's kiss
Bringing with it much passion

And the pain to part with the thought.

Art, like love, caresses the soul
to seek solace in the musings
that bring the bittersweet feelings
of being lost in a whirlwind of your own.
Art, a whisper, a shout, a dance, a song,
a warp and weft from the threads that bind,
the burst of colour or monotones of the mind.
I don't seek to define henceforth;
I merely live submerged in the passion.

Centipede's atlas

Some roads lead to places that once lived in our
minds
Some roads beckon to explore what lies beyond
Some twist like fate, not revealing what lies next
Some familiar ones stretch to places we know
best.
Where we tread the most,
we know every lamp post
And yet we find new things behind
a known turn, under a bridge or the wayside.

Roads don't really go anywhere,
but under my closed eyelids,
I see them crawling like centipedes
Joining the dots of places where I want to be.

As old as my…

As old as my boy,
Could she even cry?
Cry out the pain
Cry out in agony
Cry out the disgust
Of horrid, misplaced lust.

As old as my son,
Could she feel her life undone?
By brutality unasked for
By power unbridled
By cowardice mistaken
By morality forsaken.

As old as my child
Did she not want to hide?

Away from the struggle
Away from the fight
Away from the stench
As greedy eyes belch.

As old as my ward
Is imagining so hard?
As innocent as a bud
As playful as a brook

As old as my child
In heart, soul and mind.

Mending

A broken string of beads
That scattered like my thoughts
Some hid in corners darker than the night
Some rolled in the dust of somnolent years
Others chipped and cracked
Hurt by the reality of the hard floor.

I drew the curtains away
To let in some light
And a breeze replied to my face
Waking me from the inward glare of stillness
As the sound of the glass beads
Sends a tingling through my nerves, opening a
door.

I sweep the dark corners,
like a searchlight in a cave
And dust off the dreamy past that dulls my brain
Picking up each cracked one,
Feeling each tiny chip
I sit to string them back bit by bit.

Not all beads survived
Some changed, some stayed ingrained
In my memory, like happy afternoons
In an island's hotel room

And so, I salvage the remains
And brush them with my fingers
To feel their shape.

Eyes closed, I breathe in this feeling of
Smooth spheres of glassy hardness
The witnesses of my living
And bead by bead, I string them together
A knot here, a tug there to secure its need
In my heart and mind.

Some are reminders, some hope
Some bright, some broken,
Now the necklace is ready
With tiny globes of glimmer
And in the light of your love
They remember to shimmer.

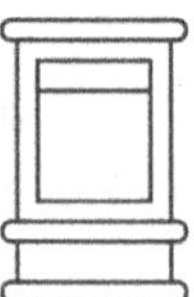

AFTERNOON SHOWERS

Tea

35

Afternoon showers on a sweltering day
Rain tree dances
Like the ripples in my steaming cup
With a breath to cool me down.

Pavement, once a shimmering haze,
Now glistens
A canvas of endless skies
Reflected in a thousand tiny eyes.

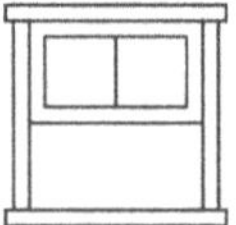

Look up

The exposed veins play hide-and-seek
with a dimpled, bumpy skin,
Legs that look more like pillars
Ending in toes, you have hardly seen.
Nothing is like it should be:
Flabby arms, thick waist
Large hips and thunder thighs
Plus-sized clothes in bad taste.

Wrinkles and folds are for clothes, not skin
Commercials peddle airbrushed dreams
Cutting apart every bit of you
It's a divide-and-rule theme
To make you feel
Like an alien in your own body.

Stop for a minute. Breathe.

Those legs walk to work
Those hips have borne babies
The laugh lines remind you of happy days
The crowfeet have seen sorrow
The flabby arms tended the sick.

You are a whole person
Not cut-up parts that need to be fixed

Embrace the imperfections
The mosaic of scars and victories
Look up from the flaws
The mirror tells the complete story.

An afternoon to spare

It's surreal what an afternoon can do
Exhilarate, refresh and renew you.
Will you feel the same another time?
For now, I rest my thoughts next to you.

You bring the sounds of your bustling life
You bring the smell of new places
You carry the ideas of a hundred souls
You gather what's around you
And pack it all in a bag of experience
Hoping it may take you to your destination.

On the way, you stumble upon
These little surprises in between
Spreading a sweet fragrance around
Like the shower of the sky jasmine.

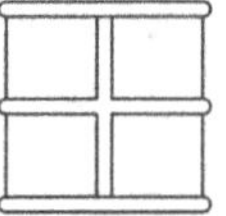

The room that smells of you

I like this floating feeling...
The room smells of you, the sheet is stained;
it's but a souvenir of an afternoon of surreal
magic.
It felt familiar and yet new,
the touch, the taste and the floating room,
Cut off from the noise of a world that won't
understand me
The way you understand my curves.

Hoping the butterflies in my tummy would cease
their chaotic dance
I sought calm in your arms;
Alas, it only heightened the nervous trance.

No, I apologise for my measured distance

When you knew and so did I
The talks were a veil to hide
What I truly felt inside
To hold you close enough to hear your heart
And feel those hands tear my soul apart
A piece of which is left in that room;
The room that smells of you.

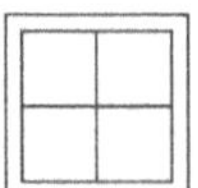

An old house

Rhythmic monotones of the rotating fan
An old bed polished to a shine
Shares with the pastel walls
Thick stories of a century bygone.

The ceiling might hide secrets of souls
Who passed on, leaving behind
The murmurs of memories
And spaces whisper into this stranger's ears
Of why the clock stopped at six.

The late afternoon sun slants into a room
Through crisscross panes
Casting shadows over the stranger's presence
Like pointing fingers at an intruder
Whose unknown fingers send shudders
Through books squeezing each other
On the creaking wooden shelf.

Among the maze of smiling faces and
Snapshots of celebrations
A deck of fortune cards asks to be read aloud
Revealing an inner voice that was asleep
On a painted iron bed with wheels.

Community

We need to stop this madness
It is spreading everywhere,
A distraught priest adjusted his orange robes.

Another one looked different
In his flowing beard
Echoing the same words with glaring orbs.

In walked another person
Clad in white, thumbing a beaded string
His speech, too, dashed all hopes.

Their chorus drowned my words of rationale
Their straitened horizons saw red
To the rainbow I offered them instead.

My banner unfurled a challenge
My madness had the strength to unite
Those who did nothing but fight.

They seek to reign with odium,
Preaching of fire and brimstone's wrath
But my rainbow's promise blazes a new path.

Two pieces of luggage

Papers, notes and garbled talk
Fill the room with words of law.
A stack of well-thumbed white
The sheets cling to each other like
Lovers soon to be separated
While a rusty staple pin loses its grip on reality.

She observes these as words turn to mumbles
and then mute in her head.
She suddenly remembers
Her home is not hers any more.
A cup appears in front of her
A meek offering of tepid comfort.

Start all over again, someone says
Those words keep ringing in her ears
Start with what?
A backpack full of her world and a worn-out
suitcase full of memories.
Her life wrapped up in two pieces of luggage
Simple to carry with space to hold on to
An address that she may someday call her own.

Social insanity

She weeps tears of blood,
Stripped of dignity, she resigns
To the brute power of the mob
That has no rationality,
no space for reason,
Only fuelled by angst
Of megalomania, otherness, and the gruesome.

Her eyes witness the scars of dirty politics,
And she tries to hide them under
The shame of her perpetrators,
Biding time till the torture ends
So she can die after taking their names.

A nation of languid eyes watches,
Senescent in their armchairs,
Before a screaming screen,
Then a flurry of fingers finds a place
For opinions and justifications
In dormant self-satisfying solace.

She cries, piercing the soul of humanity,
A playground for revenge
Becomes her body.

A deaf, blind, mute king now reigns,
Watching the spectacle, wondering
What clothes to wear next,
While a crowd gathers outside his palace.

Dirty

I hesitate to step out in the rain;
The thunder challenges me,
The wind lures me,
But I, I stay put
And refuse to get cleansed.

I refuse to let it clean my soul,
I refuse to let it wash my mind,
The grime of sins has seeped inside,
Guilt is a drug I am addicted to,
Self-pity and loathing are my drinking buddies.

If only I stepped outside
And let this cool shower calm me,

It would soothe these sores
that lie open, unhealed;
This dark mind clouded
would see clearly;
An aberration would break this chain.

I would feel the light inside
Clean in my soul,
And clear in my thoughts;
Unafraid of my dark side
If only I stepped outside.

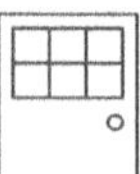

EVENTIDE

Filling up an empty cup

I lost a piece of my soul here
Among these trees, surrounded by a jungle of
brick and glass.
This lane still smells of the old tamarind tree
And squirrels still drop the fruits from a branch
or three.

Under the veil of neon lights
Lies the emptiness that most fill
With food, clothes, diamonds and cars
And I notice a swanky salon scream
'Therapy' for free when you buy a cosmetic
dream,
The irony is not lost on me.

It is my dilemma—
Should I live in this fragile nook
of the few remaining trees;
Or should I simplify my life
by going mindlessly numb
with easy consumerism?

One path takes me through nostalgia
and the complicated existence
of walking a tightrope of natural balance.
The other takes over control and puts me on

autopilot
through bright scrolling screens,
buying things I won't need,
but they satiate my greed
to hopefully fill up this emptiness inside.

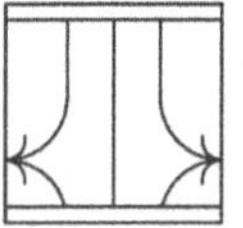

Cut the cord

I finally face my demons
My curse that I bear
For my forefathers
Like my foremothers carried.

The ink spots the white linen cloth
Spreading through the weave
Little by little, one thread at a time
Every generation, a warp
Every child, a weft
And so it spreads till nothing's left
Of the white linen
And only the stain remains.

To stop the spread
That no selvedges can end
The curse can only be contained
When the cord is cut.

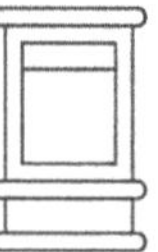

China cups in the sink

I try hard to see clearly,
but my sight can only make out
the fragile china cup slip through the soapy
hands of time,
Crash and break into a hundred problems
that I pick and seek in every nook of my brain
the tiny fragments that scattered among the
thoughts;
Their sharp edges keep pricking my mind
But I stay numb by doing the mundane.

I call it my inner zen, but really, that's a nice way
to say,
'Sorry, you are overqualified',
'We can't get back at the moment' and some such
soft blows
That hit hard and yet not so much
except to the ego of my unrequited love
for finding joy in my achievements
Till it is shattered like the china cup,
and the fragments keep hurting time and again.

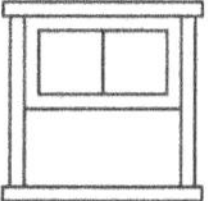

Pink

51

The attention was sidestepped
The gaping mouths ignored
No stare troubled enough to ponder
And the sly words slipped by
Just as quietly as they came.

Every day, in and out
He stomped with pride,
Taking in his stride
A secret he knew
That his shoes matched
The flowers his grandma grew.

The sights of Manora

52

Blink
The sound of the sea at Manora
The lighthouse standing tall.

Blink
On the bed, a green tube lurking around my nose
Someone walked in, I slept again.

Squeals of joy, a splash
I just jumped off Netty Jetty
The water feels cool.
The loud horn of the ship nearby,
The sound of a truck.

Beep.. beep.. beep… a new sound
My hand feels heavy
Familiar faces around me smile.
But I want to close my eyes.

Old Town smells, bazaar
I stand outside my house
I find myself in it
Playing carefree in the courtyard, I call out to
myself.

Beep.. beep.. beep…

The beeping stops,
I am inside smiling.

Forgotten umbrellas

54

It's that weather again
One where you want to
Put your feet up and
Have a book or two.

It's that weather again
One which sings to you
With the birds chirping aloud
Though it's a shade of grey for you.

It's that smell again
Of ginger tea and radio
Playing some songs from old times
Of people we left behind.

It's that sky again
That's pregnant with a storm
Waiting for the woman
To go without an umbrella
And soak her again.

It's that feeling again
Of wanting to get drenched
And getting caught in the deluge
As I walk out of the door
And forget my umbrella, happily.

Favourite colour

55

He drew a puppy
With droopy ears
And googly eyes
A curved tail to wag side to side.

The box of crayons lay before him
And he loved each one of them
So the puppy was happy
As much as a paper drawing could be
To see all the colours of the rainbow!

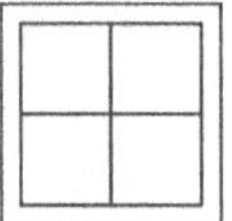

Fervent catharsis

In the silence of my study, the cursor blinks—
A mocking beacon in a sea of white,
The blank screen now stares
A taunting chasm where words fear to tread.

The keys lie cold beneath my touch,
Each letter a heavy stone in the wall of block,
The digital page, a barren landscape,
Where the echoes of deleted drafts haunt like
ghosts.

I type and see the words spilling from my head
into a cold place
That feels no grain of the hand-held diary,
No scratchy sound as the pen scribbles fervently
Across one leaf, then leaps to the next.

There is just the uniformity of the font
That was set by another as a default
Who doesn't know my handwriting
and how I like it slanted
And why it twisted the nib of my pen crooked.

I like to bend down and see the words
Scrawling along the page at an angle that hurts
my back

And yet it gives me a perspective
Like an ivy growing steadily on the fertile
riverbank.

I see my writing spreading across the page
And leaving my breath till I feel lighter.

Ageing

Youth has immense power.
How can it fathom the woes of a fading beauty?
The power to turn heads has dimmed to a flicker
of my memory,
Wisdom, instead, has made its comfortable bed.

In the moonlit night of yesterday,
I saw a reflection of lust
Today's twilight blinds me
with the reality of need.

I seek not the youth of my past,
I seek not the power to turn your heart
I merely wait for a look that will affirm my
belief
that I am still beautiful, even with my scars.

Aloneness

59

Lose yourself in the labyrinth
of a small screen with taps and dings
An escape where everything else recedes
And backgrounds blur into a homogeneous mass
of the living kind.
Random moving pictures, scrolling texts and
strangers,
Friends of a few moments
Appeasing an entirety of aloneness.

NIGHTLIFE

Last light

Last light, beautiful and foreboding
Darkness yet to slip through the cracks,
Disparages my calm mind.

Don't sleep through this dusk
Awakening isn't for the dawn alone.
Like the bats flying westwards
The evening star appears but briefly
Before being sucked into the night.

Wispy clouds tease the purple sky
A false promise
They float away with the flirting breeze
That tickles the leaves as it passes by.

A crack in time opens up
Just before the light and dark merge
I see through the crack
Into the future of my soul --
Twilight, I am you.

Reflections

62

I see her every time the grey shimmers around
my temples
Her hands are now mine,
except for the red bangles that jingled every time
she stirred the stew.
Like her, I become; unwillingly at first
And then, out of compulsion,
Her younger self is now a reflection.

In my deeds, she may find the same pain
Under the eyes,
the same shadows of a weary strife
Welcoming unwanted strangers
in dimly lit nights
Who pay pennies for an hour of skin
While I pray reluctantly amidst the chagrin.

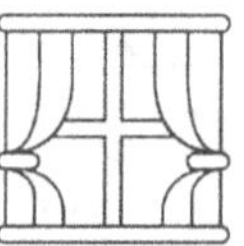

Dinner time

Each brought their own plate
Filled with thoughts
Of what would be served

Each had a smile and a worry
Of falling short of what was expected
And what they could give.

Conversation, advice, arguments
Food, water, security
War and peace;

Lambent tube lights cast faded shadows,
Silhouettes under weathered eyes
Shared stories whispered in empty spaces.

Strangers, united by circumstance,
A young girl, a torn rag doll
Hunger, not for bread.

An old man hummed a forgotten tune,
Clinking spoons and rustling clothes,
A fragile hope began to ignite.

Dinner time at the food camp
Brought tears and memories,
And humanity flickered, refusing to die. 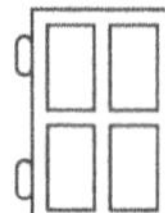

Lunatic

My full moon
That rises in me
Under the eastern sky
Of my fevered body,
Over this parched earth
Have mercy
And flow this energy
To its utmost.

Rise up through my spine
Spread through the veins
A sweet sound of the soundless
The sound of the beginning
The sound of the end
And everything in between.

My rising moon
Burn red in the twilight
Like my blood that raves
About the beauty of the womb
The creation and the destruction
And the seed of all life.

Let it settle, pray
As it throbs through my heart
And into the spaces

That remain untouched
By your silver rays.

My glowing witness
Watch me turn
Into a flower that awaits
The bee to slowly rise a breeze
through the humming wings
And I sway in the sweetness
Of the fullness of being.

Giving up the race

66

Distractions abound I was running a race
But stopped abruptly to catch my breath.

I read a book to slow me down;
The words reined in my pace,
My halt forced me to notice the grace
Of the fragrant night jasmine, the wet leaves,
the muted moonlight.
Wind rustling the palm fronds
Caressing my shameless mind.

I gave up the race of faceless crowds,
I am living with less, yet walking proud
I won't get lost in a pack,
I'll walk my own line
And admire what's around me,
To bring me back in time.

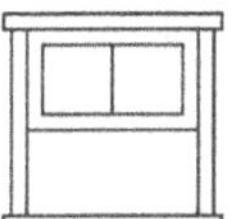

Rebirth

67

Stamps on our heads
Labels on our work
And questions on our merit.
When the blood and sweat are the same
How dare you mark us as different
From the rest that bore no brunt of the
inhumane,
How dare you identify with us.

Your sympathy is useless
As fake as the social jailhouse
That cages some for being born
Behind bars of an archaic norm.

These shackles won't hold back
A will as strong
As the ancients that claimed
That the soul will be reborn.

Hear the stars

Sometimes, I wish I could hear the stars
As they speak of other worlds from millions of
miles afar
And wonder if they can hear the cacophony of
my world's chaos
Are they too engulfed in a similar race to reach
nowhere?
Or have they better knowledge than what they
hear?

This chaos of my world is complex—
Like a thousand dreams intermingled into a
rainbow
In a simpler world, I wonder if colours exist
Or do they merge into a singularity of fact?
Is a spectrum more true than the truth of a single
beam of light that carries them all?

My questions don't cease,
they merely sleep under a blanket of humdrum
of daily life.
And yet they raise their sleepy heads when all is
quiet
And the stars are out.

I wish I could hear the stars
And know what's going on from miles afar.

Sleepwalking

I am silent
For I keep hearing the sea breeze
Singing in my ears
The song of the water lapping against the boat
The sound of my breath blowing bubbles
To the fish.

When I speak, they disappear --
The serene turtle, the graceful rays
Sea creatures of big and small shapes
Living in the blue world.
The sun that beats down on me is the same
The people I was with are here again
But the scene is different, the feeling escapes
me,
With every passing day, I go farther away.

Soon, the sea won't sing in my ears
The breeze won't brush my bare shoulders
I am landlocked and sleepwalking.
I shall wake up,
only when I am with the ocean.

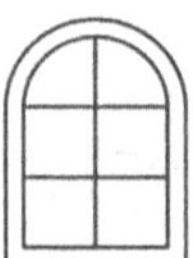

Wishes at midnight

Someone is celebrating a birthday on the street
below
Clapping, merry chatter tells me they are happy.
I know of another birthday coming soon and
another death
that makes me hollow every time I think of him.
His birthday came and went
This year, I didn't wish him
This year, he won't wish me too
Undoing is impossible, but unveiling is cathartic
Unravelling my naked self before a young
stranger
With a drink in my hand and wishing it was him.

Time for silence

It is time for silence.
The silence of a thousand souls that speak no
more
The silence of the millions who watched them
go
The silence of the earth as it lies shovelled from
a hole
The silence of ashes from last night, now cold.

Even the rain falls silently today
But some can't bear to keep quiet.

The thunder will rumble
The pyre will scream
The shovel will shift
And say what no one wishes to hear.
How many more?

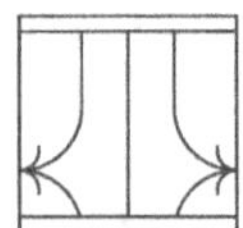

Cradling the radio

The cool breeze and radio waves
to soothe a frayed heart.
A sound from afar says hello
As I whisper, are we apart?
Songs and words
Brought warmth on cold nights.
A little window opens
As the world switches off all lights.